· CRICKET ·

FROM THE EARLY YEARS OF PUNCH

• CRICKET •

OUR CRICKET MATCH

*Smiles from the
summer game*

Special Edition for PAST TIMES® Oxford, England

First published in Great Britain by
Constable & Robinson Ltd
3 The Lanchesters
162 Fulham Palace Rd
London W6 9ER

This edition published by arrangement with Punch Ltd.

A CIP catalogue record of this book is available
from the British Library

ISBN 1-84119-196-5

Design and typeset by Tony and Penny Mills
Printed and bound in the EC

The cartoon on page 55 is included courtesy of Eileen
Brockbank. The publishers have made every
effort to trace copyright holders for cartoons
and text in this book, but they beg forgiveness
if any have been overlooked. They will
be happy to rectify this in any future editions.

PAST TIMES®

• CONTENTS •

Captain (to hurricane performer): 'Of course I should hate you to hurt anybody, Charlie, but I thought you might like to know that the fella coming in is something to do with the income-tax.'

· THE GAME'S ·
THE THING

MIDDLECOMBE v. PADDLEWICK

[1914]

I

Philip Renwick to Charles Holcombe
Room 99, XYZ Offices, Whitehall
8th August 1914

Dear Charlie, Can you possibly turn out for us on
Thursday next *v.* Paddlewick? We lost to them
rather heavily in May last and are anxious to give
them a sound beating. Their fast bowler is playing for them again, I hear, and we absolutely rely
on your help. Can you get off for the day?

Yours ever, P. R.

II

Charles Holcombe to Philip Renwick
Room 83, PQR Offices, Lombard Street
9th August 1914

My Dear Phil, Thanks for yours. Will try to manage it next Thursday, but am doubtful. My chief, though a capable official, is no sport, and I anticipate difficulties. I had a day off only two weeks ago for cricket. Will do my best. Thine, C. H.

'Turnbull, Accounts, wife sick … Hutchings, Dispatch, earache …'

III

Charles Holcombe to Philip Renwick
PQR
10th August 1914

My Dear Phil, Awfully sorry; no luck re
Thursday. Boss hopeless. I broached the matter
this morning (without actually asking for permis-
sion), but I fear the worst. You had better get
another man for the Paddlewick match. So sorry.

     Yours ever,
     Charlie Holcombe

IV

Philip Renwick to Charles Holcombe
XYZ
10th August 1914

My Dear Charlie, We shall be absolutely in the
cart without you. They've got an awfully hot fast
bowler. Bartram now tells me he can't possibly
turn out, and you are the only really decent bat I
know. We simply can't lose to Paddlewick again –
we shall never hear the last of it. No one need
know that you don't play regularly for
Middlecombe. Do try your best, old man.
Mightn't your Aunt Martha be seriously ill?

     Yours ever, Phil

Office-boy to Boss, who is off to watch an hour's cricket: 'And if anybody calls – funeral, I s'pose?'

V

Charles Holcombe to Philip Renwick (wire)

Aunt Martha dying. All well. Boss absent Thursday so can explain to him afterwards.
Holcombe

VI

Philip Renwick to Charles Holcombe (wire)

Good boy. Funeral 11.30. Train Paddington 10.5. Lunch 1.30. Draw 6.30. Philip.

VII

Charles Holcombe to Philip Renwick
Room 83, PQR Offices
14th August

My Dear Phil, I regret that I was forced to leave somewhat hurriedly after the game last night. I have nothing to add to what I told you at lunch as to the identity of the Paddlewick Spofforth with my chief, of whose sporting talent I was in ignorance. But if you should hear of a good berth going anywhere I should be extraordinarily grateful.

Yours ever,
Charlie Holcombe

PS – It was doubly unfortunate (in a way) that I should have scored a six and three fours in one over from his bowling.

• TEAM SPIRIT •

TO A BAD WICKET-KEEPER

[1926]

Air — 'Oh why do you walk through
the fields in gloves ...'

Oh, why do you stand on the field in gloves,
Missing so much and so much?
Oh, fat white booby whom nobody loves,
Why do you stand on the field in gloves,
When the air is loud with my 'Heavens above's!'
As you drop each ball that they touch?
Oh, why do you stand on the field in gloves,
Missing so much and so much?

The Charleston at Chiswick

The Tango at Tooting

IT'S ALL IN THE GAME (PART ONE)

IT'S ALL IN THE GAME (PART TWO)

' … five pounds to the National Playing Fields Association, two pounds to the Sportsman's Benevolent Society, ten shillings to the National Society for …'

THE USEFUL CRICKETER

(A Candid Veteran's Confession)

[1892]

I am rather a 'pootlesome' bat –
    I seldom, indeed, make a run;
But I'm rather the gainer by that,
    For it's bad to work hard in the sun.

As a 'field' I am not worth a jot,
    And no one expects me to be;
My run is an adipose trot,
    My 'chances' I never can see.

I am never invited to bowl,
    And though, p'raps, this seems like a slight,
In the depths of my innermost soul
    I've a notion the captain is right.

In short, I may freely admit
    I am not what you'd call a great catch;
But yet my initials are writ
    In the book against every match!

EYE-WORK: WHAT OUR BOWLERS HAVE
TO PUT UP WITH

1884
Off-side person

1904
Two-eyed person

1924
Ox-side person

For although – ay, and there is the rub –
I am forty and running to fat,
I have made it all right with the club,
By presenting an average bat!

HOT STUFF

[1945]

'IN a one-day cricket match the Delhi City Gymkhana beat the Hindu College today by 2 wickets and 64 runs at the College ground. The feature of the game was deadly bowling by Tajammul Hussain, who captured 6 wickets for 19 and who was unbeaten with 59 runs.

The Delhi City Gymkhana replied with 142 runs for 8 wickets.

At least 90 Japanese planes and 3 coastal cargo vessels were also destroyed.' – *Indian Paper*

Umpire ' 'ow do you bowl, Sir?' *Our Last Hope* 'Like Larwood.'

OUR VILLAGE UMPIRE

[1925]

IT WAS at the back of last season that Mr Hudgell, our humpire (as he pronounces it, and the aspirate certainly imparts to the word that little extra emphasis that distinguishes Mr Hudgell himself from the ordinary umpire), read a newspaper article by an eminent cricketer on the growing prevalence of the practice of making a loud and concerted appeal on every pretext, however slight, with the object of imposing upon the umpire.

Mr Hudgell cut that article out and kept it, and this

'Howt! The both of yer.'

Umpire (after answering vociferous appeal in the negative)
'That's what you get for shouting!'

season he seems to have made a firm resolve never to be biased in his judgement by the confident and stentorian tone of any appeal. And Mr Hudgell, who draws a sergeant-major's pension, is a humpire who means what he says.

Had we been aware of this resolve we should no doubt have applauded his attitude in the matter, for we ourselves had suffered often enough by reason of concerted but unjustifiable appeals. But we should almost certainly have overlooked the fact that Mr Hudgell's mind moves in certain well-defined grooves of its own.

In the first match of the season I lost the toss and we fielded. The very first ball was, to the bowler's surprise, a perfectly straight one. But the batsman mistook it for a leg-ball and stopped it with his pads. A less disputable case of obstruction could hardly be imagined.

'Zat?' bellowed half-a-dozen voices simultaneously, in no doubt whatever as to the answer.

'Nottout,' replied Mr Hudgell with great assurance.

For a moment there was silence. One could almost feel the incredulity in the air, Even the batsman had the grace to look surprised. As for the bowler –

'*Wot* did you say?' demanded Mr Hudgell, turning and facing him majestically.

Mistress 'The master is somewhat upset you should have given him out L.B.W."
Butler 'I 'ad no option in the matter, my lady. I might have overlooked a limb or two, but the 'ole body overlapped the wicket.'

'You can't intimidate *me*. I've played against worse
umpires than you.'

'I – I only said I thought–'

'Ho!' boomed Mr Hudgell, 'And oo's humpiring 'ere –
me or you?'

'You, Mr 'Udgell,' replied the bowler humbly,
retreating a few steps.

'Then I'll do the thinking.'

The general opinion was that Mr Hudgell had not been
looking, and had given the batsman the usual benefit of the
doubt. But in the next over but one the same batsman
snicked a ball into the wicket-keeper's hands. It was
unmistakable to anybody who was not both deaf and

'Ah! Now I grant you – that *is* out!'

blind. Immediately there was a confident and unanimous roar of 'Zat?'

'Nottout!' answered Mr Hudgell without hesitation.

At that point it became necessary for Mr Hudgell to leave the pitch in order to ask certain of the home spectators if they wanted something for themselves, and during his absence the fielders gathered together and hinted darkly at corruption.

But of course the fault was not in Mr Hudgell's integrity, but in his logic. Having read that nowadays many quite unjustifiable appeals were concerted and confident, he had reasoned that all concerted and confident appeals must be unjustifiable. It is not only on the physique that twenty-one years in the army leave their mark.

A certain theory formed itself in my mind, and I resolved to test it. Pretending not to notice the general astonishment and consternation as I took the ball, I put myself on to bowl at Mr Hudgell's end.

Fortune favoured me at once. The batsman – who had no moral right to be batting at all – chopped my first ball with his bat on to his pads. Of course nobody appealed, and I turned to Mr Hudgell with an assumption of diffidence, and asked in a low, almost apologetic tone.

'Er – how is that?'

'Hout!' roared Mr Hudgell.

'Who wants to stop in all day during this delightful weather?' asks a correspondent. Quite a lot of batsmen is the answer.

17 August 1938

THE
• GREEN FIELDS •
OF ENGLAND

LORD'S!

There's a glorious sanctum of cricket,
Away in the Wood of St. John;
No spot in creation can lick it
For the game at which Grace is the 'don'.
Though Melbourne may claim a Medina
The 'Mecca' of cricket must be
In the beautiful classic arena,
The home of the 'old' M.C.C.

Home, sweet home of the M. C. C.,
Ever my fancy is turning to thee!
Up with King Willow and down with the dumps
Hark to the rattle of leather and stumps.
Oh, what a rapturous thrill it affords!
Give yourself up to the magic of Lord's.

• THE VILLAGE GREEN •

A 'FIRST-CLASS FIXTURE'
[1899]

OUR OWN cricket correspondent is spending his holidays in Slocombe, a village in the depths of the country. During his stay there he witnessed a match between Slocombe and the neighbouring hamlet of Mudfield. From force of habit he felt compelled to write an account of it, which reads as follows:

Old King Sol was on his best behaviour for this important occasion. Jupiter Pluvius being in temporary abeyance. The announcement ran that the upright sticks would be implanted in the grassy sward at 2.30, but it was nearly three o'clock when, Slocombe having won the toss, its first two wielders of the willow emerged from the pavi—from the bar of the 'Red Lion'. These were the sexton and the postman, both batsmen of great reputation. Doubtless they would have wreathed their brows with fresh laurels on the present occasion, had not the sexton been given out l.b.w. in the first over on the appeal of long-leg, while the postman, in skilfully playing back to a half-volley contrived to disorganise the symmetry of his timber-yard. However, on the vicar and his gardener being associated at the wickets, a magnificent stand was made. Not until ten runs would

Why does the Press photographer confine his reports to first-class teams when the lesser lights provide such excellent material?

have been registered on the telegraph-board – if there had been one – was the reverend gentleman dismissed for a carefully-compiled four, consisting of two leg-byes (described as 'it's off the foot' by the Slocombe umpire, and so credited to the batsman), and two singles.

After his dismissal a spell of quiet play succeeded, the most noticeable feature being some smart fielding on the part of a cow grazing round the pitch, which received the ball full on her side, thereby depriving the batsman of a couple of runs. The Mudfield bowling was very deadly,

'Hey Sam, I've given 'ee guard three times.'
'I knows, George, but I stand this way to fast uns.'

Wife of Deep Field 'No, darling, Daddy can't talk to you now; wait until he's dropped this one!'

and two of the Slocombe batsmen retired hurt. Just, however, when a 'rot' appeared imminent, the blacksmith came to the rescue with a fine display of hitting, and when he was at last dismissed by a smart catch at extra-longstop he had amassed no fewer than eight runs. Thanks largely to this dashing innings, the Slocombe total reached twenty-two. After a somewhat lengthy interval the players returned from the 'Red Lion', and the Mudfield team took possession of the wickets. Their men shaped exceedingly well, and hit the bowling to every part of the field where there happened to be some one who could hold an easy catch. However, their score rose steadily, and eighteen runs had been compiled – including a five, four of which were due to overthrows – when there were still three wickets to fall. At this critical point the Slocombe umpire came to the rescue, and by his masterly decisions enabled his side to secure a glorious victory by no fewer than three runs. He had a splendid analysis, working out at seven appeals, five distinct untruths, and seven wickets

THE VILLAGE STANCE

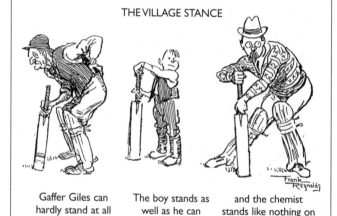

Gaffer Giles can hardly stand at all

The boy stands as well as he can

and the chemist stands like nothing on earth

• THE FRONT LAWN •

'Uncle Frank, when you made that hundred against
Yorkshire was it with a hard ball?'

• THE BEACH •

'Why not declare and put them in before tea?'

· RAIN ·
STOPS PLAY

WET-WILLOW

A Song of a Sloppy Season

Air— Titwillow

In the dull, damp pavilion a popular 'Bat'
   Sang 'Willow, wet-willow, wet-willow'
And I said 'Oh! great slogger, pray what are
   you at.
   Singing, Willow, wet-willow, wet-willow?'
'Is it lowness of average, batsman,' I cried;
Or a bad "brace of ducks" that has lowered
   your pride?'
With a low-muttered swear-word or two
   he replied,
   'Oh willow, wet-willow, wet-willow!'

'Want me to mention the weather for Saturday's cricket?'

He said 'In the mud one can't score, anyhow,
    Singing willow, wet-willow, wet-willow!
The people are raising a deuce of a row,
    Oh willow, wet-willow, wet-willow!
I've been waiting all day in those flannels – they're damp!
The spectators impatiently shout, shriek, and stamp,
But a batsman, you see, cannot play with a Gamp,
    Oh willow, wet-willow, wet-willow!

Now I feel just as sure as I am that my name
    Isn't willow, wet-willow, wet-willow,
The people will swear that I don't play the game,
    Oh willow, wet-willow, wet-willow
My spirits are low and my scores are not high,
But day after day, we've soaked turf and grey sky,
And I sha'n't have a chance till the wickets get dry,
    Oh willow, wet-willow, wet-willow!!!'

37

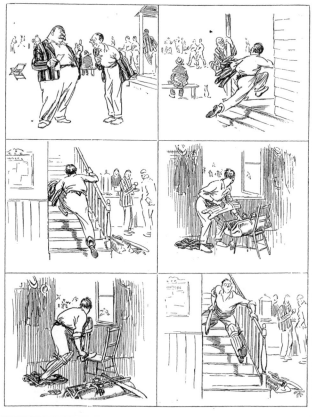

THE CHANCE OF A LIFETIME

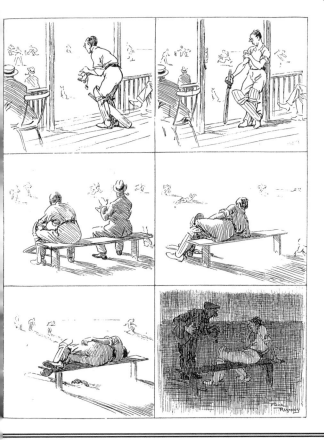

• REFRESHMENTS •

THE TEA INTERVAL
[1903]

ON THIS most important feature of first-class cricket much can be said. In the old benighted days, when the most noteworthy figures selected for hero-worship were the Graces, A. G. Steel, C. T. Studd, A. N. Hornby (to name these only), luncheon was the only meal partaken of during a match. Bearing this fact in mind, it is of course no matter for surprise that cricket was what it was – a pastime almost wholly neglected by the newspapers, creating no popular interest in the County Championship, offering little employment to photographers or statisticians, and with hardly a single first-class player criticising in print the matches in which he took part.

Fortunately we have changed all this, and the game has now taken its right place in the affairs of the country. On inquiring into the cause of this salutary alteration, by which the cricketer has become a public character, second in fame only to a music-hall artist, we find that it

'I'm getting too old to play captain's innings, but thank goodness I can still eat a captain's lunch.'

synchronises with the introduction, so long and danger-
ously delayed, of the tea-interval

In the advance of the cricketer from the monophagous
to the biphagous stage, the scientific historian of the game
will not fail to note the advent of the crowning phase of its
evolution. What was once a monotonous display of animal
endurance, lasting from a quarter to three to half-past six,
is now pleasantly broken at half-past four by an adjourn-
ment to the pavilion for a cup or cups of the refreshing bev-
erage of China, Assam or Ceylon. Tastes differ in this matter, as in everything else. Mr C. B. Fry finds Orange Pekoe
with a dash of Oolong the most stimulating variety, not
only for the game but for the many literary labours con-
nected with his innings. Mr P. F. Warner prefers a syrupy
Souchong. Mr Jessop is a pronounced adherent of
Gunpowder. Prince Ranjitsinhji favours a blend of Indian
leaves. Mr Maclaren swears by pure China with a slice of
lemon in it. Mr H. K. Foster will not look at cream. Albert
Trott, curious to relate, prefers brown to lump sugar.

It is pleasant for the historian to be able to record that
cricketers are reviving some of the graces and amenities
with which tea was taken in the days of Pope. Now and
then, it is true, one is distressed to see a professional
pouring the steaming liquid into his saucer; but for the
most part the exponents of the game of games (as it has
been called) empty their cups with charming delicacy
and *espièglerie*. And this reminds us that some very dain-

ty porcelain services are now to be seen in the County pavilions, which vie with each other in a friendly contest of ceramic taste. Sussex is famed for its Sèvres, and the Wedgwood set at Old Trafford has not its equal in the kingdom. On the other hand it is an open secret that the inadequate tea-table equipment of one of the Midland Counties nearly led to the discontinuance of several of their most attractive fixtures. The difficulty, however, has been happily surmounted by the princely munificence of a local magnate, who recently presented the County Club with a superb service of Crown Derby, a set of apostle spoons, and twelve exquisitely embroidered hem-stitched tablecloths.

· WOMEN ·
AND CRICKET

THE LADIES AT LORD'S

OLD STYLE – EARLY 1860s

SCENE – *The Ground and its Accessories*

Superior Creature Really very pleasant.

Weaker Sex Oh! charming. So delightful having luncheon *al fresco*. The lobster salad was capital.

S. C. Very good. And the champagne really drinkable.

W. S. And our chat has been so interesting, Captain Smorltork.

S. C. So pleased. And now, what do you think of the cricket ?

W. S. Oh! I haven't time to think of the cricket.

'My dear child, do you realise you walked across
behind the bowler's arm?'
'Oh, I know him awfully well. He won''t mind.'

Mere Man Really rather nice.

Stronger Sex Quite nice. Capital game, too. Up to county form. That last over was perfect bowling.

M. M. Yes; and the batting was well above the average.

S. S. Tol-lish. And really, when I come to think of it, Mr. Smorltork-Gossip, you have been also most entertaining.

M. M. Proud and honoured. And now, what do you think about the luncheon?

S. S. Oh! I haven't time to think about the luncheon.

'And look here, young Peter – if you play with us we don't want any schoolgirl stuff.'

THE MARTYR OF CRICKET
[25.4.1874]

In this case of breach of promise £2000 damages were awarded. The only reason the gentleman could give for breaking his engagement, was that the lady did not take any interest in cricket.

Liverpool Assizes: Law Report: Stevenson v. Eccles

'Not care who bat, or bowl, or field.'
    Growled Eccles to his conscious pillow,
'I'll teach the maid, who will not *wield*,
    That she instead must *wear*, the willow.'

'The man shouted "Over!"'   'I know, dear, but the thing goes on.'

But Miss to lose this Lord demurs,
  Who for Lord's pastime disregarded her:
And so twelve anti-cricketers
  Two thousand damages awarded her.'

With tears of pride, Elevens, beweep
  This mulcted martyr to the game:
His memory, like your wickets, keep,
  Oval and Lord's – his earliest flame!

In wives may he yet make a catch –
  Find some *Grace* worthy of his worth –
And when found, may they play a match
  For life, of Cricket on the Hearth!

'Tom and Alison spent *their* honeymoon in the Bavarian Alps ...'

· SPECTATOR ·
SPORT

from
THE CURSE OF CRICKET
[1912]

WOOLLEY stepped out and leaned against the ball, and it shot past cover to the boundary. This is the sort of cricket I can enjoy quite easily by myself, but the man on the bench below was afraid I might be feeling lonely. He turned round and introduced himself with the remark, 'They're using the long handle.' When a stranger says that to you at Lord's, you know at once that your day is spoilt. You can get up and leave the ground, or you can stay and talk to him; you can't watch cricket anymore.

'Yes, they're taking the long handle to it this morning,' he said again.

'Why are they doing that?' I asked innocently.

'They want to declare, you see; that's what it is. Oh, well fielded, Macartney. That's Macartney, that little fellow at mid-off. It won't be like this when Australia goes in,' he said. 'They'll play for keeps.

'I once saw Sutcliffe drop one like that.'

'They ought to play for something,' I agreed.

'I don't know about Macartney. He generally goes for the gloves.'

'Yes, we must get him to go for those if we can.'

'Wonderful bat, Macartney. He's the only man who's made a thousand runs, you know.'

'Fancy!' I said. 'A thousand! Is he really the only man who's ever done it?'

'This year, of course.'

'Oh!' I tried hard to keep the disappointment out of my voice, but I am afraid he noticed it.

'You'd never think a little chap like that could hit the ball so hard,' he went on. 'It's timing, that's what it is — all timing. Look at Jessop.'

'But I thought he wasn't playing.'

'Ah, and why isn't he? They never ought to have left Jessop out. If I were a selector, I should always say, "Give me Jessop, and then you can put in who you like."'

'Then I should put in Carruthers. He made a century for Leamington once. And he bowls too — slow benders.'

'But that's Fry all over. He's a bad captain. Why doesn't he declare now? We've got 300 on the tins.'

'Perhaps he hasn't noticed it,' I suggested.

'Some people call him a good bat, but I don't. Not What I call first-class. Good against bad bowling, but no good against the best.'

'Like me.'

I should always make Warner captain at Lord's. He knows every blade of grass on the ground.'

'By name?' I asked with interest.

'And then Warner knows the Australians.'

'Ah, well, there's not so many *of them*.'

'You see — Well fielded, Smith! Fielded, sir! That's Smith; he's a great footballer.'

'I thought he was a wicket-keeper.'

'Oh, that's our Smith. The Australians have got a Smith playing too.'

'Are they relations?'

'They've taken your advice, dear. He's changing the bowling

'Pooh, sir, you should have felt Jessop.'

'Not that I *know* of,' he said as though allowing that they might have arranged some thing privately. 'There! Fry's declared at last. Now the Australians have got to sit on the splice for the rest of the day. The question is, can they do it?'

He asked this so fiercely that I didn't like to give an opinion. 'Just as you think,' I said modestly.

'Well, *I* say it depends how the wicket rolls out. If it doesn't roll out easy, and if Fry has sense enough to start with Barnes and Foster –'

'There is certainly a resemblance, but am I right in saying Grace was somewhat taller.'

'Barnes and Warner, surely?' I said. 'Because if Warner knows all the different blades of grass and all the different Australians –'

He looked at me with compassion. 'Warner doesn't bowl,' he said kindly.

'Don't see much cricket, do you?' he added.

'I'm afraid I don't get as many opportunities as I should like,' I said truthfully, for there are black days in the week when I have to stay away from Lord's and work.

'I thought p'r'aps you didn't. Now I've watched it for

54

thirty years. Ever seen Grace?' he asked with the air of one who had an anecdote to tell.

'I don't *think* so,' I said. 'What's he like?'

And that gave it away'. He looked at me with sudden suspicion, and then slowly reddened. He turned away and buried himself in his paper. But his spirit was undaunted. A newcomer took the seat next to him, and my friend, having taken a glance out of the corner of his eye, introduced himself.

'I suppose,' he said carelessly, 'they'll play doggo?'

A.A. MILNE

'... two hundred and eighty-seven for two wickets!'

· CLOSE OF ·
PLAY

THE CRICKETER IN WINTER
[1903]

The days are growing short and cold;
    Approaches Autumn, ay and chill Yule;
The latest bowler new has bowled
    His latest devastating pillule.
Gone are the creases, gone the 'pegs';
    The bungling fieldsman now no more errs
By letting balls go through his legs
    And giving batsmen needless fourers.

Things of the past are drive and cut,
    With which erstwhile we would astound men;
The gay pavilion's doors are shut;
    The turf is given up to groundmen;
Gone is the beautiful length-ball,
    Gone, too, is the batsman who would snick it;
Silent his partner's cheery call.
    Football usurps the place of cricket.

'First it was horticulture, then it was statues, and now all he can
think of is cricket!'

Now, as incessantly it pours,
    And each succeeding day seems bleaker.
The cricketer remains indoors,
    And quaffs mayhap the warming beaker.
Without, the scrummage heaves and slips;
    Not his to play the muddied oaf. A
Well-seasoned pipe between his lips,
    He reads his *Wisden* on the sofa.

Or, if in vein for gentle toil,
    Before he seeks a well-earned pillow,
He takes a flask of linseed oil
    And tends his much-enduring willow,
Feeling the while, what time he drops
    The luscious fluid by degrees on,
Given half-volleys and long-hops,
    How nobly it will drive next season!

'No bridge tonight, I'm afraid. He's at work on a system
for getting Bradman out.'

Then to his couch, to dream till day
    Of fifties when the pitch was sticky,
Of bowling crisply put away,
    Though it was manifestly tricky,
Of umpires, confident appeals,
    Hot shots at point, mid-off, and cover,
Of cricket-lunches (perfect meals!):
    Such dreams attend the cricket-lover.

Hollowood

'Try a faster one, dear – I think he's beginning to get the hang of it.'

AT HOME
The Cricket Enthusiast

And, though the streets be deep in snow,
    Though slippery pavements make him stumble,
Though rain descends, though blizzards blow,
    It matters not: he scorns to grumble.
What if it lightens, thunders, hails,
    And common men grow daily glummer,
In him contentment never fails;
    To such a man it's always Summer.

FIELD OF VISION

In shades of grey to suit his choice
   His little kingdom glows;
Booms loud or soft that kindly voice
   To tell him what he knows;
For him the scoreboard's fleeting view,
   The ash tray on the floor,
The coffee brought by people who
   Creep out and shut the door.

'Just a little to leg, dear.'

THE CRICKETER'S GRAVESTONE

'Our Sheffield Correspondent telegraphs: An extraordinary tombstone dispute has arisen at Wadsley Bridge, near Sheffield. The widow of one Benjamin Keeton, a recently deceased cricketer of some local renown, has erected a tombstone to her husband's memory, on which is carved a set of stumps, about a foot high, with bat and ball. The vicar and church-wardens declare the stone was surreptitiously fixed, and have ordered its removal, which has caused intense local excitement.'

Pall Mall Gazette, December 1876

O Wadsley Bridge, where Keeton bloomed,
  Thy vicar's wits what ails?
To bowl the stumps of Keeton tombed,
  Estreat his buried bails!

Could Keeton plead, to his life's fame
  He'd urge the symbols german,
More home, than to some parsons came
  Prayer-book, and bands, and sermon.

That hit, and all, he now must waive,
  Score closed, runs run, green-swarded;
Alas! he cannot guard his grave,
  As his mid-stump he guarded.

But why disturb the symbolled stone
    Above this quiet sleeper,
Who with his life's score fairly shown,
    Must face Heaven's wicket-keeper?

Dying, perhaps he thought, 'If he's one
    As is fit to keep wicket,
He'll know a cricketer when he sees one,
    And hand me my gate ticket.'

'Clean blowed. Well, I'm bowled.'